MW01244927

Tidings of Comfort and Joy

A Family Christmas Album

❦ Tidings of ❧
Comfort and Joy

A Family Christmas Album

Museum of Fine Arts, Boston

Mystical Marriage of St. Catherine (detail)
Pieter de Witte

RIZZOLI
NEW YORK

Front cover illustration:
Botticelli (Alessandro Filipepi called Botticelli), Workshop of
Italian (Florentine), 1444/45-1510
Virgin and Child with the Young Saint John the Baptist
Tempera on panel, 48¾ x 33¼ inches
Sarah Greene Timmins Fund
95.1372

First Published in the United States of America in 1992 by
Rizzoli International Publications, Inc.
300 Park Avenue South
New York, NY 10010 and
Museum of Fine Arts, Boston
465 Huntington Avenue
Boston, MA 02115

Project coordinators: Kathryn Sky-Peck and Susan Carpenter
Designed by Christina Bliss

ISBN 0-8478-5643-7

92 93 94 95 96 / 10 9 8 7 6 5 4 3 2 1

Printed and bound in Hong Kong

Contents

Hymn

Lord when the wisemen came from far
Led to thy cradle by a star
Then did the shepherds too rejoice
Instructed by thy angel's voice
Blest were the wisemen in their skill
And shepherds in their harmless will.

Wisemen in tracing nature's laws
Ascend unto the highest cause
Shepherds with humble fearfulness
Walk safely, though their light be less
Though wisemen better know the way
It seems no honest heart can stray.

There is no merit in the wise
But love (the shepherds' sacrifice)
Wisemen always of knowledge past
To the shepherds' wonder came at last
To know can only wonder breed
And not to know is wonder's seed.

A wiseman at the alter bows
And offers up his studied vows
And is received. May not the tears
Which spring too from a shepherd's fears
And sighs upon the frailty spent
Though not distinct be eloquent.

'Tis true the object sanctifies
All passions which within us rise
But since no creature comprehends
The cause of causes, end of ends
He who himself vouchsafes to know
Best pleases his creator so.

When then our sorrows we apply
To our own wants and poverty
When we look up in all distress
And our own misery confess
Sending both thanks and prayers above
Then though we do not know, we love.

Sidney Godolphin
1610 (?) – 1643

Introduction

Christmas is a joyous time, a family time when relatives and friends gather together in celebration. It is a time of delicious food and delightful entertainment that often passes much too quickly. This family Christmas Album is a four year journal to record your holiday thoughts and memories. Beautifully illustrated with Medieval and Renaissance paintings that tell the Christmas story, this album is also a keepsake book. It is meant to be passed along in your family, allowing others to fondly remember the decorations, special foods and beverages, gifts, and carols of each of the holiday celebrations recorded.

We hope that this Christmas album becomes a part of your family's holiday tradition. May it provide you with many hours of enjoyment, both in its compilation and its re-reading.

Two Angels, Piero di Cosimo

Holiday Family and Friends

Adoration of the Magi, Workshop of Bartholome Zeitblom

Holiday Food and Spirits

_____

_____

_____

_____

_____

_____

_____

_____

_____

_____

_____

_____

_____

_____

Holiday Gifts

Madonna and Child, Luis de Morales

16

Favorite Christmas Memories

_____

_____

_____

_____

_____

_____

_____

_____

_____

_____

_____

_____

_____

_____

_____

_____

Archangel Gabriel
Master of the Miraculous Annunciation of Ss. Annunziata

18

Scenes from the Life of Saint John the Baptist (detail)
Master of Saint Severin

Coronation of the Virgin, Master of Bonastre

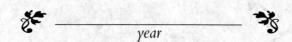

Virgin and Child Enthroned with Angels, Neri di Bicci

Holiday Family
and Friends

_____

_____

_____

_____

_____

_____

_____

_____

_____

_____

_____

_____

_____

_____

_____

_____

Virgin and Child, Bramantino

Holiday Food and Spirits

Holiday
Gifts

Jeremiah with Two Angels (detail), Gherardo Starnina

❦ _____

_____

_____

_____

_____

_____

_____

_____

_____

_____

_____

_____

_____

_____

_____

_____

Angel of the Annunciation, Martin Schongauer

Favorite
Christmas Memories

_____

_____

_____

_____

_____

_____

_____

_____

_____

_____

_____

_____

_____

_____

_____

_____

_____

_____

_____

_____

_____

_____

_____

_____

Jeremiah with Two Angels , Gherardo Starnina

Virgin and Child with the Young Saint John the Baptist
Workshop of Botticelli

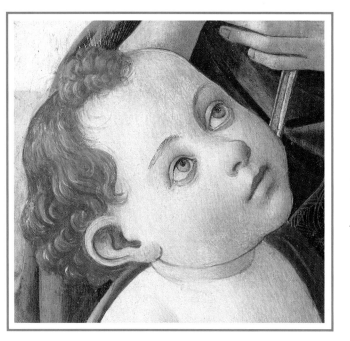

Holiday Family and Friends

✤ _____

_____

_____

_____

_____

_____

_____

_____

_____

_____

Nativity, Martin Schongauer

Holiday Food and Spirits

_____

_____

_____

_____

_____

_____

_____

_____

_____

_____

Virgin of Humility (detail), Giovanni di Paolo di Grazia

Holiday Gifts

Saint Luke Painting the Virgin, Rogier van der Weyden

Favorite Christmas Memories

_____
_____
_____
_____
_____
_____
_____
_____
_____

Virgin and Child with Saints Jerome and Anthony of Padua and Two Angels, Francesco di Giorgio

47

Adoration of the Magi, Tintoretto

Symbol of St. Matthew, Martin Schongauer

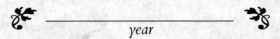

Flight into Egypt, Master of the Schretlen Circumcision

Holiday Family and Friends

_____

_____

_____

_____

_____

_____

_____

_____

_____

_____

_____

_____

_____

_____

_____ ❧

_____

_____

_____

_____

_____

_____

_____

❧ _____

Saint Matthias and Saint Matthew
Master of the Holy Kinship

Holiday Food and Spirits

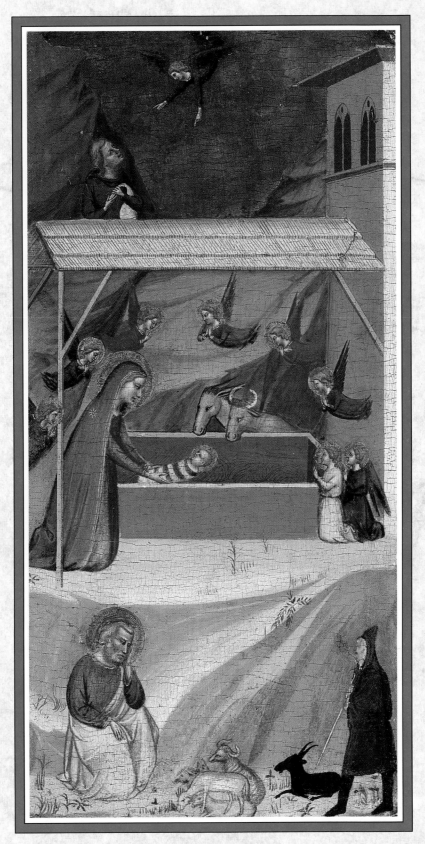

Nativity, Bernardo Daddi

Holiday
Gifts

_____
_____
_____
_____
_____
_____
_____
_____
_____
_____
_____
_____

Virgin and Child, Master of the Saint Barbara Altar

Favorite Christmas Memories

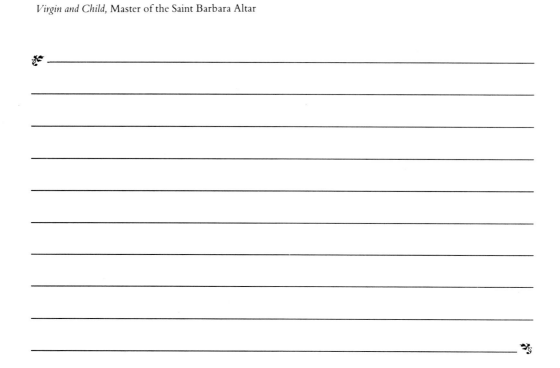

Virgin and Child, Lippo Memmi

Virgin Adoring the Child, Sebastiano di Bartolo Mainardi

The Three Genii, Albrecht Dürer

Family
Holiday
Photographs

The Annunciation (detail), Giuliano di Simone

Assumption of the Virgin
Niccolo di Ser Sozzo Tegliacci and Workshop

75

The Archangel Michael, "Peregrinus"

Index

Memmi, Lippo
(Filippo di Memmo, called Lippo Memmi)
Italian (Sienese), active 1317–1347
Virgin and Child
Tempera on panel, 29¾ × 21⅞ inches
Charles Potter Kling Fund
36.144

Luis de Morales
Spanish, about 1509–1586
Madonna and Child
Oil on panel, 18⅛ × 13⅝ inches
Gift of Misses Aimée and Rosamond Lamb
1978.680

Giovanni di Paolo di Grazia
Italian (Sienese), active about 1420–died 1482
The Virgin of Humility (detail)
Tempera on panel, 21⅞ × 16⅝ inches
Maria Antoinette Evans Fund
30.772

"Peregrinus"
(presumably Pellegrino di Giovanni di Antonio)
Attributed to Italian (Perugian), active 1428
The Archangel Michael
Tempera on panel, 39⅜ × 14⅝ inches
Charles Potter Kling Fund
68.22

Schongauer, Martin
German, before 1440–91
Angel of the Annunciation
Engraving
Gift of Mrs. Lydia Evans Tunnard
63.2876

The Nativity
Stephen Bullard Fund
19.1453

Symbol of St. Matthew
Engraving, 3⅝ × 3⅝ inches round
Horatio Greenough Curtis Fund
44.606

Guiliano di Simone
Italian (Lucchese) active 4th quarter, 14th century
The Annunciation, detail from *The Crucifixion
with the Virgin, Saints John and
Mary Magdalen and Two Donors,
and the Annunciation*
Tempera on panel,
32⅜ × 18¾ inches overall;
design area 27 × 14⅜ inches
Seth K. Sweetzer Fund
22.403

Starnina, Gherardo
Italian (Florentine), 1354–1409/13
Jeremiah with Two Angels (detail)
Tempera on panel
Gift of Mrs. Thomas O. Richardson
20.1857

Niccolò di Ser Sozzo Tegliacci and Workshop
Italian (Sienese), active 1334–1363
Assumption of the Virgin
Detail from *The Death and Assumption
of the Virgin with Saints Augustine,
Peter and John the Evangelist and a
Deacon Saint; and Christ Blessing with David,
Saint John the Evangelist, Solomon
and Ezekial*
Tempera on panel. Overall: 104⅜ × 84½ inches
Center panel, from which detail is taken
78 × 34⅜ inches
Gift of Martin Brimmer
83.175b

Tintoretto, Domenico
(Domenico Robusti, called Domenico Tintoretto)
Italian (Venetian), 1560–1635
Adoration of the Magi
Oil on canvas, 57⅞ × 116⅛ inches
Hebert James Pratt Fund
26.142

Rogier van der Weyden
Flemish, about 1400–1464
Saint Luke Painting the Virgin and Child
Oil and tempera on panel
53⅛ × 42⅝ inches
Gift of Mr. and Mrs. Henry Lee Higginson
93.153

Pieter de Witte (called Pietro Candido)
Flemish (worked in Florence and Munich)
about 1548–1628
The Mystical Marriage of St. Catherine (detail)
Oil on canvas, 89 × 62⅝ inches
Henry H. and Zoë Oliver Sherman Fund
1980.72

Zeitblom, Bartholome, Workshop of
German, 1455/60–1518/22
Adoration of the Magi
Oil on panel with fabric ground
62⅜ × 40⅞ inches
Gift of Mr. and Mrs. Frederick Starr
50.2720